SAN FRANCISCO
IN COLOR

SAN

Profiles of America

FRANCISCO

in Color

TEXT BY T. H. WATKINS

HASTINGS HOUSE · PUBLISHERS
New York

The text is dedicated to Elaine, Lisa and Kevin—
and to Hutch, who opened many doors

PUBLISHED 1968 BY HASTINGS HOUSE, PUBLISHERS, INC.

Revised Edition, 1970
Reprinted January, 1973
Reprinted February, 1976
Reprinted August, 1977

All rights reserved. No part of this book may
be reproduced without written permission of the publishers

Published simultaneously in Canada by
Saunders, of Toronto, Ltd., Don Mills, Ontario

Library of Congress Catalog Card Number: 68–16004
ISBN Number: 8038–6645–3
Printed and bound in Hong Kong by Mandarin Publishers Limited

CONTENTS

6

PART ONE

The Bonny, Merry City . . .
The Good, Gray City

I

WHY SHOULD ANY reasonable man become captivated by a city? At best, cities have always been crowded, dirty, noisy, badly planned and worse constructed, hamstrung by inadequate transportation and ridden by all sorts of civic, social and physical problems. It would seem that the genius of man might have provided some better way to live with himself.

In spite of all the obvious disadvantages, the history and traditions of many of the world's cities have produced a curious amalgam that denotes romance, adventure or what-have-you—some intangible quality of mood that captures the imagination and stirs the blood. It is not easy to resist the pull of a name like Paris or London, Rome or Acapulco, a fact that has not escaped the attention of travel agents and airlines. This is the Age of the Instant Tourist; wanderlust has become big business and, aided by all the computerized tools of technology, a man can slake his thirst for the faroff at the drop of a credit card. More often than can be counted with any accuracy, he slakes it in San Francisco.

San Francisco is one of the very few American cities to exude an attraction comparable to that of venerable European capitals. Most self-respecting American cities have active Tourist Bureaus, promotion facilities and a powerful grasp of their own significance, but few come close to capturing the appeal of San Francisco—an appeal that would probably exist even if the local Chamber of Commerce, in a moment of madness, launched a vigorous campaign to eliminate the tourist trade (worth several millions of dollars annually). San Francisco's appeal to the tourist has existed in full flower almost from the date of the city's birth. Since the gold rush of 1849, San Francisco has entertained a steady stream of the great, near-great and perfectly ordinary types who have come to see for themselves what it is all about.

The state of urban America in the middle of the nineteenth century may have had something to do with the formation of San Francisco's charisma. At the time of the gold rush, the great cities of the East already were beginning to foreshadow the agonies of the future. Boston, for more than a century the most vigorous, enlightened city in America, was taking a back seat commercially, and in spite of a literary flowering that made her the intellectual Athens of the East, would soon find herself slipping into a combination of Back Bay provincialism and wardheeling corruption. New York City, with a population that topped 350,000, could not be denied its financial leadership, nor could it be denied that it already harbored an incredible, crawling warren of the dispossessed; ghetto was not yet an American word, but in New York City it was a desperate reality. Philadelphia, ostensibly inclined to brotherhood, still carried the physical and psychic scars of religious war; in 1844, the city's Irish Catholics and an organization of Protestants styling itself the Native American Party had clashed in some of the most vicious rioting in American history. Grandly designed Washington City was a jerry-built, pestilence-ridden town where fine sentiments wafted down from Capitol Hill and money changed hands swifter than the eye could follow, where back-scratching was already a refined art and the lobbyist reigned supreme.

This dismal picture in no way represents the whole of American life in these years; there was vigor and opportunity aplenty left in the country, as well as a healthy portion of honest idealism. Still, it was becoming obvious that Jefferson's fine Arcadian dream of free, prosperous men living in a harmony uncluttered by the antagonisms and poverty of the Old World was being revised violently by the Industrial Revolution and the pressures of an increasingly complex age. It would be misleading to suggest that San Francisco and the gold rush came along at this time as a kind of historical convenience, or that it would not have been much of a gold rush without the impetus of crowded Eastern cities, widespread unemployment, disillusion and general social ferment. It is not impossible, however, that much of San Francisco's inherent appeal stemmed from an inarticulate feeling that here, in this instant city by the western gate, crawling with young, lusty types from all over the world, full of excitement and promise—that here it could all be made to work. The city never has quite lost that unwritten promise.

II

THE GENESIS OF the city took place in 1776, when a Spanish explorer-captain named Juan Bautista de Anza led 240 soldiers and civilian colonizers north from Hercasitas in Sonora via Mission San Gabriel and established the sites of what would become Mission Dolores and the Presidio of San Francisco. For more than fifty years these two miniscule outposts of civilization were all there was of San Francisco. Today, both have been nicely restored and together comprise the only tangible link to what has been called the city's "Spanish Heritage".

That heritage was supplanted, if not noticeably enlarged, in 1822, when Mexico declared her independence from Spain and took over California. But the central government in Mexico—like that of Spain before her—was just too far removed to have much telling effect on social evolution in California. San Francisco's Presidio and Mission simply drifted through most of the first half of the nineteenth century, awash in splendid isolation. By 1836, when Richard Henry Dana described the scene in *Two Years Before the Mast*, the Spanish and Mexican heritages combined had produced something that fell a bit short of metropolis: "Beyond . . . were dreary sandhills, with little grass to be seen, and few trees, steep and barren, their sides gullied by the rain. Some five or six miles beyond the landing-place [Yerba Buena Cove], to the right, was a ruined Presidio, and some three miles to the left was the Mission of Dolores, as ruinous as the Presidio, almost deserted, with but a few Indians attached to it. . . ."

Even as Dana wrote, however, the city had legitimately begun. William A. Richardson, an English sailor late of the British whaler *Orion*, had arrived in the area in 1822 and taken up permanent residence. The energetic Richardson purchased a pair of waterlogged schooners, repaired them and launched a trading enterprise that was soon expanded to include the servicing of whaling vessels that entered the Bay in search of wood, water and other necessaries. In a short time, Richardson had become the region's leading entrepreneur, and one of the marks of his success was a board-and-batten shanty on the shores of Yerba Buena Cove, erected in 1835. Two years later, he added another, and as the California authorities gradually relaxed their formerly rigid trading restrictions, Richardson's tiny commercial complex took on the form of a village called Yerba Buena, its name derived from an herb native to the area.

Over the next several years the village grew slowly, but with admirable consistency, as its population was nourished by a collection of such "Yankee" merchants as Jacob Leese and William Leidesdorff, who served the needs of a steady trickle of American immigrants who crossed the Sierras and settled in the rich bottomlands of the Sacramento and San Joaquin valleys. By the time of the Mexican War in 1846 (by which little exercise we acquired not only California, but territory that later comprised most of the states of New Mexico, Arizona, Utah, Colorado and Nevada), Yerba Buena was a viable little seaport well prepared for American military and commercial possession. The transfer of control from Mexican to American hands took place with a minimum of fuss. On July 8, 1846, Commodore John D. Sloat, commander of the Pacific Fleet, ordered Captain John B. Montgomery of the U.S.S. *Portsmouth* to take possession of Yerba Buena. Montgomery led a landing party ashore, raised the American flag, declared the village the official property of the United States, and the *Portsmouth* fired a twenty-one gun salute, the most belligerent aspect of the whole proceedings. Conquest over, spectators retired to a local saloon and hoisted a few in commemoration, the beginning of one of San Francisco's oldest and most respected traditions. About six months after these festivities, Washington A. Bartlett, Chief Magistrate of the town, proclaimed that "the name of San Francisco shall hereafter be used in all official communications and public documents or records appertaining to the town".

Yerba Buena had become San Francisco; a city was born.

III

"SAN FRANCISCO IS A mad city—inhabited for the most part by perfectly insane people," Rudyard Kipling once said. The British poet and novelist visited the city in 1889, when it was at its apogee of vigor, and while his statement can be passed off in part as the typically disdainful opinion of a man not noted for his democratic inclinations, it came very close to the truth. Moreover, if he had said it forty years earlier, it would still have rung true.

The city was the child of madness. Founded on a finger of land 3000 miles removed from what was generally described as civilization, the city was one result of a madness called "Manifest Destiny", which precipitated the Mexican War and made it possible to appropriate half a continent. Established on that lunatic base, San Francisco was given its greatest push toward glory by another—one of the most asounding manifestations of national insanity ever experienced by any country anywhere: the gold rush.

In January of 1848, when the city was still a scattered collection of improvised homes and businesses with a population of considerably less than a thousand, laborers discovered significant quantities of loose gold on the American River, about 150 miles northeast of the town. News of the discovery was some time in filtering down to San Francisco. Sacramento Valley land baron John A. Sutter, whose employees had found the gold, managed to keep it secret for a while, theorizing (quite correctly) that his land, already invaded by squatters of one kind or another, would be overrun if the news got out. Since he was not a stupid man, Sutter made a hurried attempt to obtain title to the land on which the gold had been found but it did him little good. During February, rumors of gold drifted down to San Francisco, and as evidence of its existence became more and more convincing, residents of the town began slipping out in twos and threes.

The gold rush was as yet no more than a trickle, but when a canny entrepreneur by name of Sam Brannon, who happened to have a little store going up near Sutter's Fort, not far from the diggings, came stamping into town in the middle of May shouting, "Gold! Gold! Gold on the American River!" and waving a bottle full of nuggets over his head, the town emptied. Employees quit, bartenders offered one on the house and galloped off, crews deserted their ships in the Bay, often followed by their captains. Those few merchants left in town chortled gleefully as they experienced a run on picks, shovels and other paraphernalia declared suitable for getting at gold; and when their supplies were gone, they counted their money, shrugged and took off for the hills themselves. While inadequate records make it impossible to ascertain precisely how much gold was mined by these " '48ers" in the spring and summer months—when the gold rush was still a *local* affair—conservative estimates place the figure at not less than $6,000,000, and it was probably more. This was no speculator's fabrication—it was the real thing.

It became a national experience in December 1848, when President James K. Polk put the government's stamp of approval on the whole business: "The accounts of the abundance of gold . . . are of such an extraordinary character as would scarcely command belief were it not corroborated by the authentic reports of officers in the public service. . . ." Enterprising Yankees needed no more. The traveling months of 1849, 1850 and 1851 saw one of the most stupendous mass migrations in human history. In 1849 alone, it is estimated, at least 40,000 streamed across the continent, and thousands more by sea, and while the flood abated in 1850 and 1851, it was enough to swell the population of California from 12,000 in 1847 to more than 100,000 in 1852, by which time the former western outpost of the Spanish Empire had become a full-fledged American state.

IV

ONE OF THE EARLIEST arrivals to this new El Dorado was New York reporter Bayard Taylor, who gave a good account of the effect of the gold rush on the little village called San Francisco: "Hundreds of tents and houses appeared, scattered all over the heights, and along the shore for more than a mile. . . . On every side stood buildings of all kinds, begun or half-finished, and the greater part of them were canvas sheds, open in front, and covered with all kinds of signs, in all languages. Great quantities of goods were piled up in the open air, for want of a place to store them. The streets were full of people, hurrying to and fro, and of as diverse and bizarre a character as the houses. . . ." Growth displayed hothouse characteristics, and just four months later Taylor could report the addition of balconied hotels, solid warehouses and *haut monde* restaurants. "San Francisco seemed to have accomplished in a day the growth of half a century."

Unfortunately, most of it burned down at one time or another during six major fires between December 24, 1849, and June 2, 1851. Many of these were attributed by the victims to the city's growing population of potential jailbirds, and while the allegation has never been proved it is entirely possible. Looting was doubtless easier when the city was in flames, and the directness of the whole business would have appealed to the simplicities of the criminal mind. For some, proof was unnecessary: "It seems useless to write and talk to the people of San Francisco," the editor of the *Alta California* wrote after the June fire of 1851. "They have lost all resentment. They love to be burned out. They seem to have set it down as one of their luxuries. It is something *recherche*. We look with apparent satisfaction upon the sprightly attempts of the recruits of penaldom to illuminate our city free gratis."

The editor's disgust was understandable, but not altogether justified. A number of the city's more respectable types finally became so fed up with the fires, the crooked elections, the generalized corruption and vice, that they decided to take matters into their own hands in a move that established a precedent for the periodical *ad hoc* justice that popped up all over the West in later years. They formed a Committee of Vigilance in the summer of 1851, expeditiously hanged three criminals, scared out a significant number of others and, by giving all incoming ships a careful perusal, were able to refuse entrance to many others. While the ethics of such procedures might not bear close scrutiny, they tended to work; with the point made clear, the Committee ceased operations after ten weeks. It was not revived until five years later, when conditions again became so bad as to indicate immediate action. This time, the Committee functioned for three months, deported twenty-five certifiable felons, ordered and encouraged the exodus of nine hundred more and with all deliberate speed hanged four others. After the spring and early summer's work, the Committee disbanded officially and forever. Shortly afterward, concerned citizens got together and elected what historians have often considered one of the best administrations in the city's history—although this may not qualify as an unreserved compliment, given the nature of the general run of city administrations.

V

By the end of the 1850s, San Francisco had reached a kind of maturity. The hysteria of the gold rush, with its frantic construction pace, its economic and social chaos and its floating populations of disappointed miners who had discovered that gold, for some unforseen reason, did not lie around on the ground where it could be had with a long-handled shovel—most of this had long since passed. While the city could still furnish "the best bad things that are obtainable in America", her coltish beginnings seemed to have been replaced by a solid, if lively, period of progress and prosperity and a citizenry fated to stay and grow with the country in the standard American fashion.

San Francisco was saved from this stolid future by the second of those cataclysmic developments on which the city seems to have taken out a patent. Silver in astounding quantities was discovered in western Nevada, some 220 miles to the east. This was the incredible bonanza of the Comstock Lode, and San Francisco's financial Establishment was not long in staking out an almost uncontested claim, soon becoming the chief supplier of the Nevada mines and miners and the central clearing-house in all matters concerning stock speculations, sales and outright swindles.

She was one of the richest cities in the world by then. Her own gold mines still produced an impressive tonnage with the aid of advanced technology; a rapidly growing wheat industry presaged the day when California would be the most productive agricultural state in the nation; manufacturing of any and all kinds flourished in the city itself; and her fishing trade already was showing signs of the gargantuan enterprise it would become. To all this had been added the steady stream of wealth from the Comstock. Small wonder, then, that the city did not exactly throw herself body and soul into the agonies of the Civil War. To San Franciscans, the Great Rebellion was an exciting but relatively unimportant distraction from the main order of business, which was the making of money and more money. Such detachment from a national crisis was easy enough to maintain, for the city was isolated from the rest of the country in every way imaginable: 2000 miles by land, 18,000 by sea and even far away in spirit; not even the Pony Express, begun in 1860 and capable of delivering the mail from St. Louis in a little over ten days, was much of an antidote to the isolation. San Francisco was alone out on the far edge of the continent; her interests were her own, her concerns her own.

Even as the Civil War ground to a deadly halt, however, forces were at work to end that superb detachment. Ever since a visionary by the name of Asa Whitney had first proposed the idea back in 1845, the concept of a transcontinental railroad had festered in the American consciousness. And what a grand idea it was—to lay 2000 miles of track across man-killing deserts, thundering rivers and alplike mountain ranges—so grand that it had to be irresistible. The Civil War made it apparent that the idea was not only grand but necessary, and so an about-to-be-very-rich group of California transplants—Collis P. Huntington, Charles Crocker, Leland Stanford and Mark Hopkins (forever after known as the Big Four) went into action. They organized the Central Pacific Railroad, wangled out of a not very reluctant Congress the most astounding land giveaway in the history of the country, were joined in the enterprise by an Eastern organization called the Union Pacific, hired droves of industrious Chinese and began to build themselves a railroad.

The Union Pacific started west from Omaha, the Central Pacific east from Sacramento; on May 10, 1869, the rails of the two companies were joined at Promontory, Utah. In San Francisco, where the significance of the event was joyously recognized, bells rang, whistles blew, citizens gamboled in the streets, champagne and good Irish whisky flowed and, in a typical spasm of chauvinism, some marched through town with a banner proclaiming: *San Francisco Annexes the United States!*

The physical isolation was at an end, but the spiritual isolation that had been bred and nurtured over the previous twenty years would remain.

VI

IN THE THIRTY-SEVEN years between the completion of the transcontinental railroad and the earthquake and fire of 1906, San Francisco forged the basics of her image. No longer an overnight wonder vulnerable to the fickle winds of boom-and-bust, she was solid, if not particularly respectable; vigorous, if not always level-headed; colorful, provided one defined "color" in terms broad enough to include a healthy slice of unmitigated depravity; enthusiastically opulent to an extent that made her the archetype of conspicuous consumption long before the term was even invented; and as totally self-conscious as any city on earth.

Probably nothing more aptly typified the solidity, vigor, color, opulence and self-consciousness of these gilded years than the story of the splendiferous Palace Hotel of William C. Ralston. Ralston, who had come to San Francisco in 1851 and scrambled up the financial ladder with skill, persistence, foresight and luck, was grateful for what the city had done for him and determined to pay it back in kind. His Bank of California, fattened by the wealth of the Comstock mines, funded one project after another designed to enhance the city's financial, social, cultural and esthetic leadership west of the Mississippi.

The Palace Hotel was meant to be one such project. Construction began in April of 1874, and by the time of the hotel's grand opening in October, 1875, it had cost the Bank of California $6,000,000. This immense, seven-story 800-room monolith on the corner of New Montgomery and Market streets stood as the most inescapable monument to San Francisco's affluence for more than thirty years; princes and presidents came to stay and gape. It embodied in its stone and marble hulk all the hopes and possibilities of the city. It served its calculated purpose well until its destruction in 1906, and "Billy" Ralston would have considered it worth every cent of the six million dollars.

At the time of its opening, Ralston was dead. His Bank of California, stretched thin by too many grand projects, could not survive a hysteria-produced run in August of 1875; it failed, and on the day after it closed its doors William C. Ralston took a swim in the Bay.

The story of the Palace and its founder is a particularly striking suggestion of the city's golden era (and one of the favorite stories in her memorabilia), but the time and the city were made up of many things—some splendid, others not. Making up a significant part of the splendor were the Nob Hill mansions of the Bonanza and Railroad Kings, so grotesque they verged on the beautiful—Jim Flood's massive brownstone cube with its $30,000 brass fence kept glittering, the crenelated wonder of the Mark Hopkins home, gray and towered and turreted, the Crocker mansion, the Colton mansion, the Stanford mansion—superb monuments to bad taste gotten out of hand, tributes to an age in which money was meant to be seen as well as heard.

Splendid, too—like a fetid corpse dressed in finery and on its way to the Lick House Ball—was the Barbary Coast, a rough square mile bounded on the Bay side by East Street, on the south by Clay and Commercial, by Broadway on the north and Chinatown on the west. Here was the capital of wickedness west of the Mississippi—and perhaps east as well. The sins of the Barbary Coast provided saloon and parlor conversation across the country and over the world; these sins were past belief, rumor had it (moreover, rumor was quite right). Here was the domain of the crimp, who doped, mugged and shanghaied the sailing man for fun and profit, making it possible for a man to stop in for a quick one and wake up the next day bound for Tasmania. It was a welter of prostitution, where everything from saloons to restaurants provided the ways and means, and lurid dance halls the inspiration, if needed. The girls trafficking in this trade represented as cosmopolitan a spectrum as you might find anywhere in the world: dewy-eyed farm girls from Fresno worked side-by-side, as it were, with delicate Chinese and aging French professionals, with Chileans, Peruvians, Negroes and Cockneys. If there was a sin the Barbary Coast hadn't committed, it was only because there was no money in it, and in a style not peculiar to America this enclave of whoredom, drunkenness and murder became one of the great tourist attractions of its time, rivaling the iniquitous dens of the original Barbary Coast from which it had taken its name.

Chinatown was another section of the city suited for the titillation of proper matrons from Philadelphia and the smug outrage of visiting clergy. It was a slum with the glossy finish of the picturesque. First drawn to California in the gold-rush years and later imported in large numbers to provide cheap labor for the construction of California's half of the transcontinental railroad, the Chinese of San Francisco had clustered in a ramshackle section west of the Barbary Coast. In this district, about six blocks long and two wide, some 30,000 human beings lived in Dickensian squalor and cultural alienation from the land and the time in which they existed. Here the gaping tourist from the East could wallow in the sight of tenements hardly less crammed and rickety than New York City's finest, and certainly more colorful; he could tour opium dens and the rank cribs and alleys where even children practiced a trade as old as time itself; and if he were lucky, as Rudyard Kipling was in 1889, he might even witness the murder of a man in a murky gambling den.

The aura of romance provided by the city's enclaves of sin and squalor was dubious at best, but the sense of adventure she gained from the sea that surrounded her was real. Her Bay was one of the great natural harbors of the earth, and through the Golden Gate streamed a steady cross-section of world trade: stained, element-beaten tramp windjammers in from Liverpool and Le Havre; steam schooners loaded to the scuppers with lumber from the green hills of the high Northwest; ships packed with copra from the South Seas, tea from China, mahogany from the Philippines, silk from Japan, coffee from South America; Chinese junks, international whalers, the codfishing fleet of the Alaska Packing Company, redolent with the stink of crops from northern seas. The crews who manned these ships from the far and near horizons were a sea-going United Nations: blond Norwegians and black Gilbert Islanders, Chileans and Peruvians, Kanakas from Hawaii, Tlingits from Alaska, Greeks, Chinese, Japanese, Russians, Cockneys, Scots and a multitude of others. To this frenetic study in world commercialism were added the vessels of internal commerce: the ferries leaving broad wakes between Bay cities, scow schooners with thirty-foot deck stacks of hay from the Sacramento delta, fleet little sloops of the oyster fishermen, revenue-cutters and pilot boats and—a startling touch of the Mediterranean—the orange-brown lateen sails of the Italian fishing fleet.

This, then, was "The bonny, merry city—the good, gray city" memorialized by reporter Will Irwin, who remembered it as "The gayest, lightest hearted, most pleasure loving city of the western continent. . . ." A mosaic of contrasts, a city of wealth and poverty, startling beauty and stupendous ugliness, robust life and squalid death, romance and commonplace, Latin exuberance and Oriental detachment, skepticism and optimism. A city of life, light and enchantment.

And on the morning of April 18, 1906 the good, gray city died.

VII

"AT 5:15, I WAS awakened by a very severe shock of earthquake. The shaking was so violent that it nearly threw me out of bed. It threw down a large bookcase in my chamber and broke the glass front; another bookcase fell across the floor. The bric-a-brac was thrown from the mantel and tables and strewed the floor with broken china and glass. . . ."

Thus did a local businessman describe in a few understated words the San Francisco earthquake of 1906. The San Andreas fault, a primordial crack that runs nearly the full length of California, had made a minor ninety-second adjustment in its alignment, a matter of ten feet or so, and its shrug set off a disaster that ended in the death of a city.

Damage had been widespread and dramatic in that ninety seconds; rubble littered the streets, chimneys were dismantled, windows shattered and whole walls of residences and public buildings alike simply disappeared into dusty piles of clutter. Even so, the destruction was not so bad that it could not have been repaired in a short time. After the initial hysteria, San Francisco counted heads and thanked their sundry gods that it had been no worse.

And then the city began to burn. Broken gas lines, shredded electrical connections, overturned stoves, ruined water facilities and the city's predominant wooden architecture combined to transform what might have been an unfortunate incident into a genuine catastrophe. Not even New York City's Wall Street fire of 1835 or the great Chicago Fire of 1871 could match the ravaging effect of San Francisco's armageddon—not to mention its drama, as one observer reported it: "From Gough Street, looking down, we saw the great tide of fire roaring in the hollow toward Russian Hill; burning so steadily for all it burned so fast that it had the effect of immense deliberation; roaring on toward miles of uninhabited dwellings so lately emptied of life that they appeared consciously to await their immolation; beyond the line of roofs, the hill, standing up darkly against the glow of other incalculable fires, the uplift of flames from viewless intricacies of destruction, sparks belching furiously intermittent like the spray of bursting seas."

After three days of backbreaking effort, during which it seemed at times the fire would go on forever, the flames were contained, then controlled. By then, however, they already had annihilated four square miles of what, to all intents and purposes, had been the city of San Francisco—514 blocks containing 28,000 buildings; the loss totaled an estimated $350,000,000. Four hundred and fifty people had died; the cost of their lives was not estimated. The city was a smoking maze of snags and rubble, black shells, contorted steel frameworks. It presented a landscape out of nightmare, but one looks at the hundreds of surviving photographs of this period of the city's agony with a shock of recognition. We have seen it all before—Hamburg, Berlin, London, Warsaw—all the shattered cities of World War II; San Francisco's ruin was a peculiarly twentieth-century landscape

It did not stay that way long. With a vigor of which the city has been legitimately proud for sixty years, rebuilding began even before the smoke cleared. Within three years, more than a third of the destroyed city had been reconstructed, and by 1911 her recovery was so unarguably complete that she won Congressional approval as the city chosen to commemorate officially the completion of the Panama Canal with a world's fair. The city fell to with classic enthusiasm, filling in a 635-acre stretch of tidelands between Fort Mason and the Golden Gate and erecting on the site an impressive array of miniature palaces and landscaped gardens—and a small-scale replica of the Canal itself. The Panama Pacific International Exposition opened for business on February 20, 1915. It was a smashing success; diplomats and statesmen (and such politicians as William Jennings Bryan) came to view with approbation and point with pride, and by the time the Exposition closed in December of the year, nearly 19,000,000 visitors had flocked the grounds. Upon the closing, the Exposition site suffered a modern fate: the filagreed palaces (with the exception of the Palace of Fine Art, preserved and recently restored), lavish gardens and open courtyards were razed and demolished; streets were laid out and houses and apartments sprang up in what is today known as the Marina District, an enviable place in which to live.

San Francisco had survived her disaster with a vengeance, making an effective bid on the glories and incongruities of the twentieth century. If she has since displayed a certain air of smugness about it all—illustrated by the self-endowed sobriquet of "the city that knows how"—it is not difficult to forgive her.

VIII

THE HALF-CENTURY following the Exposition would provide its share of the city's excitements, including the Preparedness Day bombing of 1916, the desperate General Strike of 1934 and a four-year madness called World War II, social disorders as typical of the city's story as any other phenomenon (and no one who has survived the experience of a wartime liberty town would care to call war anything *but* a social disorder). More in keeping with the city's "go ahead" heritage, however, were the two Bay bridges of the 1930s. Begun in 1933 and completed in 1936, the San Francisco-Oakland Bay Bridge was an engineering wonder that spanned more than eight miles of open water by utilizing Yerba Buena Island as a leapfrogging agent to the East Bay. The Golden Gate Bridge, shorter but always somehow more impressive, took six years to build, opening for business in the spring of 1937. The city's ever-present willingness to celebrate her own ingenuity was then reflected in another world's fair, the Golden Gate International Exposition of 1939.

It would be unwarranted to imply that the city that had been built up on the ashes of the earthquake and fire, then swollen by the disruption of the Second World War and further revised by the complex forces of the 1950s and 1960s was the same that had given birth to all the legends of her golden era. It was not, yet the complicated welter of emotional and psychological attitudes that made up her birthright was not destroyed by fire, nor completely altered by time and circumstance. Like a middle-aged matron recalling the vigorous charms of a former lover, the eye of the city's heart has always been on her sometimes lurid but always compelling past. This affection has enabled her to avoid taking the twentieth century too seriously; it has given her the antique courage that tolerates the different without hysteria—"a century-old thread of humanism," columnist Herb Caen has called it, "that comes of being thrown together with all kinds of people on a tiny spit of land at the Western edge of a continent".

The more San Francisco changes, the more she is the same. The past is not dead; it is alive and well on the windy crest of California Street, where a man can stand and look down into the innards of an indisputably modern city, yet catch a hint of the wild, free optimism that may have been the essence of the American Dream.

PART TWO

Notes of a Vagabond Tourist

I

THE HISTORY OF my own love affair with San Francisco began more than fifteen years ago on the flat, dry plain of the San Bernardino Valley in Southern California. I must have been fifteen or sixteen years old when rumors of a shining white city full of great things happening came to my callow ears. Being a typical adolescent, I was ready to believe every myth I encountered, and I encountered plenty while wallowing in the literature available in the local library. As the years passed, I managed to develop a certain sophistication and even a kind of native skepticism, but neither had the slightest effect on my green and glorious theories regarding San Francisco.

These theories included, among other things, the belief that the city was populated almost exclusively by women beautiful enough to make strong men clutch at the corks of their brandy bottles; great poets and novelists who turned out masterworks in grand little apartments on Telegraph Hill while watching Tahiti-bound schooners slip in and out of the Golden Gate; businessmen who drank with epicurean style and read Plato in their off-hours; and newspapermen who cultivated a cynical wisdom between coverage of stupendous ax-murders and anti-graft crusades. Obviously, this magnificent congeries would provide the atmosphere wherein a man of creative bent could live with the vigor of a Jack London, the elan of a Lucius Beebe and the fiscal serenity of a Louis Lurie. I vowed at an early age to become part of it all, and even before graduation from college began an epic prose poem in way of preparation.

The poem was never finished, but I did make it to San Francisco a very few years later, a totally senseless, badly planned move that I have never once regretted. I had no job waiting for me, less than $100 in pocket, no place in which to live, and I knew precisely two people in all the vast Bay area. Moreover, I was not alone; with me were one patient wife, two infant children and one neurotic dog. With admirable disregard for straitened circumstances and distorted convictions, we rattled up the beautiful Coast Route in our dispirited automobile, hauling behind us a trailerful of worldly possessions.

We clattered through Santa Barbara, dozing in the sun like a little old lady in a beach chair; through the green mushroom hills around San Luis Obispo; through the Steinbeck country of the Salinas Valley, dry and yellow and somehow vague around the edges; through San Jose and north on the Bayshore Freeway past row upon row of pastel housing developments and factories that seemed to deal exclusively in electronic gadgetry; past clusters of motels and restaurants surrounding International Airport; past San Bruno Mountain, an upstart hillock that would not impress a resident of the Rockies; and finally, through a rolling series of brown hills mantled with little white houses sitting shoulder-to-shoulder like a regiment of troops.

I have learned since that there are no bad ways to enter San Francisco, but for a time after my first entrance, I was convinced that none could possibly match the drama of that first sight of the city from the south, thrust upon us as we rounded the shoulder of one last hill. For the moment, at least, all my elusive expectations were made real: the city *was* gray and white and quite magical, and if for a moment I felt a little like Dorothy skipping off after the shimmering façade of Emerald City, I've never experienced much chagrin on account of it. The saccharine perfection of that first impression didn't last forever, of course. I soon found it was no easier to write the Great American Novel in San Francisco than in any other city; nor was it much easier to feed growing children and a hungry wife. I learned, too, that San Francisco had its pockets of ugliness, its monumental inconveniences and all the other agonies common to mid-twentieth-century urban America. But one curious fact remains: in spite of an increased knowledge of the city and its problems, in spite of a familiarity that might have bred contempt, I've never shaken the adolescent crush that led me here. Like some adenoidal lout yearning after the town's "fast" girl in a modern novel of bad manners, I contemplate San Francisco through an affectionate haze that tends to blot out imperfections.

II

IF A MAN truly is serious about a love affair, he'd better be prepared to work at it with the diligence of a leg man for the Internal Revenue Service. Love's rewards are manifold but the price is high, there being a good deal of sweat involved in the whole business. At least, that is what the manuals say, and while I don't consider myself qualified to comment on the truth of that contention in regard to people, I personally can guarantee its applicability to the matter of man-city relationships. I fell in love with San Francisco a long time ago, and have been working like hell at it ever since.

The main difficulty has been one of getting to know her. She is not a big city, but her complexities are astounding. The city is a maze of wonders and curiosities, and even though it became obvious shortly after I began my personal investigation that there was no way to learn it all, there was a fascination in the quest that soon was the only motive needed. I became a professional tourist, a vagabond taking in all the standard Chamber of Commerce delights of the city, but also poking my nose into oddball corners and shadowy crannies, watching, enjoying, understanding less than I should have, learning more than I might have expected. Much of the time, I simply got lost, since I possess probably the most poorly developed sense of direction west of the Mississippi and north of a given point. I probably have gotten lost in San Francisco in as many different ways as possible—and there are plenty of ways. Such incidents of aggravated disorientation may or may not have broadened my knowledge of the city, but they definitely have enriched it with details I might not have encountered otherwise.

Ranging as it has from the dogged, wide-eyed probing of the enthusiast to the purely accidental discoveries of the native bumbler, my investigation of the city over the past several years has been unorthodox and probably naive. Nevertheless, it has reinforced me in the conviction that San Francisco is my own, my native city and has given me the gall to make sweeping generalizations about it with the best of them. None of which makes it one whit easier to answer the question implied—but so far avoided—in this narrative: exactly what *is* San Francisco? The question is legitimate enough but almost impossible to answer with any real certainty. San Francisco, like a good-looking woman or the best of modern art, is all things to all men—from the superficial to the profound.

Some time ago I gave a personally conducted tour of the city to a pair of relatives from Los Angeles. They are good people and openminded, but possessed of the Teutonic skepticism of the long-time Angeleno, who has learned to live without a city to love. At first, the tour was an unmitigated disaster. Taking them first to Union Square in the early evening, I tried to convey my feeling that here was the quiet eye of San Francisco, an oasis surrounded by mighty hotels and big and little shops, where the night air is punctuated by the insistent clangor of cable cars and one can best hear (and feel) that strange, amorphous murmur that is produced by the functioning of any living city. They were not impressed; as a matter of fact, they said, Union Square rather reminded them of downtown Los Angeles. Very similar. Being a person of restraint, I did not push them in front of a passing truck.

At that point, as an uncooperative fate would have it, a San Francisco summer gale came whipping over Nob Hill, converting Powell Street into an Arctic wind tunnel. The cable cars that came our way were jammed, and looking down to the foot of Powell Street, I could see that hundreds of tourists were waiting to board others. A cable-car ride was going to be impossible, obviously, so I hailed a passing taxi to take us up to the Fairmont Hotel and its outside elevator (that would impress them, I knew). Climbing to the top of Mason Street, one of the city's most heartstopping inclines, an overloaded cab ahead of us stalled at the crest of the hill, its rear wheels having encountered a slick spot on the street. We sat perched on the hill while the livid cabdriver ahead fruitlessly spun his wheels. The rank odor of burned rubber mingled with the sea wind. My relatives kept glancing back over their shoulders, as though they were clinging to the lip of a cliff with their fingernails.

"Don't look down," I said helpfully. "They say it helps if you don't look down."

They laughed without conviction.

Finally, after he had emptied the cab, the stalled driver managed to edge it over the crest of the hill, and we proceeded to the Fairmont—and discovered that the outside elevator was out of service. The lobby of the hotel was packed with a Saturday-night crowd waiting to take the other elevators; the situation was the same across the street at the Mark Hopkins. It would be at least half an hour before we could get a ride to the top of either hotel.

Cursing under my breath, I led them out of the hotel and into a local bistro, where we sat glumly awhile. Feeling they ought to have at least one pleasant reminder of the evening, I announced that we would walk back down to our car parked in the Union Square underground garage. San Francisco is a walking man's town, if ever there was one, but I had forgotten that my relatives were Southern Californians, a religion in which the automobile is the single most important tool of worship and the act of walking an unpopular heresy. They were grimly game, however; the girls removed their high-heel shoes and we all trooped down Powell Street—or what I assumed was Powell Street, not having bothered to check. I discovered when we had finally stumbled down to the foot of the hill that we had in fact been on California Street, a miscalculation that meant several more blocks of walking before reaching Union Square. There wasn't a taxi in sight, so I led them on, and on, and on. They did not say anything, but I knew they were convinced that I had been trying to cripple them.

The next day, in a move conceived in desperation, I drove them across the Golden Gate Bridge (I would have liked to walk, but hadn't the nerve to suggest it) to Vista Point, a shelf of land carved out of the Marin headlands, and popular for the view it provides. This time everything worked. The Bay and the city were putting on the kind of show that has enriched the coffers of picture-postcard manufacturers for decades. The air was crisp, clean and cool, with just enough wind to feather the top of an occasional wave and the kind of light that lends a startling clarity to everything. In the far north end of the Bay a regatta was making up, a stunning collection of brilliant white sails. A freighter cooperatively steamed under the Golden Gate Bridge, itself looming redly and impressively to the south. And the city was gorgeous, acting for all the world like a woman who had performed slatternly the night before and was trying to make up for it. My relatives gasped, exclaimed and snapped pictures right and left; it was a highly successful afternoon. They returned to the Southland with an affectionate remembrance of at least one San Francisco—and if their picture-postcard San Francisco was not quite the city I had hoped they would learn to love in the course of their two-day excursion, it beat a poke in the eye with a sharp stick.

III

THE PRECEDING VIGNETTE illustrates what may lie at the heart of San Francisco's appeal: the ability to reproduce herself in multiple forms, like something seen through a prism turning slowly. The city is an urban kaleidoscope, shifting in color, mood and meaning from section to section, day to day, even hour to hour. Sometimes the change is purely physical, an effect produced by the quality of light at the moment. The city seen from Vista Point that summer day, preening herself in the bright, windswept air, was a startlingly different city from those I have seen on other days, in other lights. Often, the change is stunningly dramatic, as on the day I watched her after a late-afternoon storm while driving across the Bay Bridge. The storm was breaking up; great, thick shards of clouds hung high west of the city. Through them, the light of the sun was filtered to a mellow red flush, striking the still wet streets in flat reflections and giving them the appearance of canals. The city took on a soft, roseate light and became a vision of Venice transported, something Walt Disney might have worked up for a scene in *Fantasia*. The vision ended the moment the sun was blocked by a hulking cloud; the city was suddenly gray and dim, as somber and uninviting as a landscape out of *Wuthering Heights*.

Such sudden shifts in appearance are typical of San Francisco, and doubtless affect what it is that men feel for her. The drama of moments like this is fleeting and superficial, but a city that is liable to change personalities on you in an instant is a city to be reckoned with.

San Francisco displays the same fickleness in less metaphysical ways. I have called her an urban kaleidoscope; perhaps it would be more accurate to say that she is an immense grab-bag from which a man can sample a startling variety of delights and incongruities available in one of the few American cities that is not yet strangling in its own inadequacies. Here he can feel a strong link to the knowable past while keeping an uneasy eye on the barely comprehensible present and catching a hint of the inscrutable future. Here he can still find islands of grace and serenity in a sea of raucous modernity —and if these zones of diversity and mood are not necessarily unique to San Francisco they are uncommonly sharp and eminently available.

Market Street, a wide slice out of the heart of downtown, provides a short but memorable lesson in the varieties of time and style accessible to the vagabond tourist. In days not so bygone that use of the term has disappeared, Market Street was known as "The Slot", a description derived from a cable slot that once ran down the middle of the street. It neatly bisects two wildly divergent areas of the city: "South of the Slot", a landscape of warehouses, hock shops, job-printing plants, garages, ghastly little pensioners' hotels, scabby bars, used-office-furniture emporiums and parking lots; and the north, an enclave featuring the commercial castles of the corporate rich, the home of banks and stockbrokers, department stores and bookshops, where even the drugstores have carpeting on the floors.

Beginning at the Ferry Building and sauntering south, you can take a twenty-minute walk on Market Street through the past, present and future, through vistas of bad taste and elegance, extemporaneous style and calculated vulgarity. The Ferry Building is a part of the past. Built in 1903, it survived the earthquake and fire uncommonly well, although the clock in its tower stopped at the hour of the earthquake and remained so for a year. Until the two Bay bridges made the ferries obsolete (for a time), passengers flocked through its yellow-cream walls twice a day, every day, by the thousands, the city's first commuter population—a floating population, as it were. Now only the offices of the San Francisco Port Authority and the Harbor Police remain as a reminder of the building's vigorous maritime beginnings. As automobile traffic yearly swells to unmanageable proportions, some say the ferries, or their modern equivalents, will return; perhaps yes, perhaps no, but at least no one yet has successfully advocated tearing down the Ferry Building. But over it looms the undeniable present in the form of the Embarcadero Freeway, a concrete incongruity out of time and style with its surroundings.

A few hundred feet up from the Ferry Building is Marine Plaza, a miniscule park formed in the triangulation of Market and California streets, one of the many little green pockets that can be encountered in any given part of the city. Here is the headquarters building of the Southern Pacific, heir-apparent of the Central Pacific and the Big Four. The building is starkly modern (as is the business it houses), yet it is built on the site of the Preparedness Day bombing of 1916, and is a little over a block away from the site of "Fort Gunnybags", the headquarters of the Vigilance Committee of 1856. Moreover, the Plaza itself is at the terminus of the California Street Cable Car Line, which was created for the convenience of the Big Four, enabling them to ride comfortably from their downtown offices to their mansions up on Nob Hill. The past that pervades Marine Plaza has impact here—but just northwest of it is the Golden Gateway Project, a massive attempt at urban redevelopment with an unmistakable style of its own and a sense of the future.

A more successful commingling of past and present than that represented by the Ferry Building and the Embarcadero Freeway can be seen a few blocks up from Marine Plaza at Mechanics Square. This spot was once on the very shores of Yerba Buena Cove, in the years before all the filling-in and building-up, and Market Street from this point north was a wharf that ran 2000 feet into the Bay. At the northeast end of the Square is the Mechanics Monument, sculpted by Douglas Tilden and erected in 1901 as a memorial of Peter Donahue, founder of the Union Iron Works, one of the city's earliest and most successful manufacturing concerns. Of more modern monuments to commercial acumen and energy in the Square, the Crown Zellerbach Building stands as archetypical. Perhaps beautiful, definitely impressive, this shining green slab of a glass building rises into the cityscape from a perch on serpentined columns, and all around it the Square has been expanded and opened to light and air. At the lunch hour, the Square here is converted into a girlwatchers' paradise, as secretaries and receptionists from surrounding office buildings congregate on walls and benches to soak up sun, eat from brown bags (or sip at diet drinks) and indulge in universal female chatter. A grand and glorious sight, guaranteed to get a man's blood moving again and invigorate a sluggish metabolism.

Between Mechanics Square and the Civic Center, a matter of eleven blocks, the present takes over with all the clattering insistence of a discotheque in high gear. No miracle mile, this section of Market is a street of the possible and the purchasable, a garish neon wilderness where a man can buy anything from a hot dog and admission to a dirty movie to a Paris original and a bus ticket to Reno. It is all the small-town Main

Streets wrapped up into one, with all the clamoring disorganization, architectural anarchy, proud tastelessness and hopeless traffic congestion of the genre. Yet if any one section of the city can be called the "pulsing heart" of San Francisco this must be it. For it does indeed pulse, with a thick stream of people and commerce, traffic and noise; over it all there should be a monstrous, blinking neon sign proclaiming "We Never Close!"

Even here, amid the cluttered present, there are hints of the past. The Sheraton-Palace Hotel at New Montgomery is one such; it was constructed in 1909 around the shell of the fire-destroyed Palace Hotel of William C. Ralston. Here, too, is Lotta's Fountain, presented to the city in 1875 by Lotta Crabtree, an actress of the gold-rush years. It sits in splendid detachment from the bustle around it on a traffic island in front of the de Young Building, and in 1910 was the site of one of the city's fondest-remembered occasions: a street concert given by Luisa Tetrazinni, an opera star whose vocal projection must have been stupendous to satisfy the thousands who gathered to hear her in an age before microphones. A curious echo of that event can sometimes be seen at a similar island in Powell Street, where religious orators are wont to gather and bellow out the tenets of their sundry persuasions to the studied inattention of passing shoppers.

The past exists on Market's "Main Street", but it is nearly buried by the present—which itself is in danger of the future. As of this writing, construction of the Market Street subway of the Bay Area Rapid Transit system has begun. We have been told that construction will take two years; given the past record of the system's development, however (some have dubbed it the "Slowest Rapid Transit in the World"), we may assume that pile-drivers, earth-moving machines and compression drills will punctuate the clamor of Market Street for another three years, at least. And when it is finally done, planners say, Market Street will be purified and beautified, possibly even improved. Perhaps, but one is permitted a pinch of regret. For all its sometimes repelling vulgarity, its noise and shoddy signs, Market Street is moving, vital, and as unmistakably real as the front page of a newspaper with sixty-point headlines. It is now a tramway into the past, present and future, but if it is significantly changed, then part of the essence of San Francisco must inevitably be lost.

IV

A CITY IS people—not a particularly profound statement, but one that may need to be stated outright in an age of what Herb Caen has called "Plastic Inevitable", an architecture that tends to overwhelm its makers. When staring up at the impressive stretch of a modern high-rise apartment building or one more slate-sided office complex, it is very difficult to connect it emotionally with the people who designed it, built it, or those who must use it. For all their mongrel architectural styles, pointless ornamentation, misuse of space and general lack of comfort and practicality, there was no mistaking the fact that the skyscrapers of the early decades of this century were conceived, constructed and utilized by people. They mirrored the foibles of an age in which a skyscraper was a celebration of man's ingenuity, not a comment on his anonymity.

San Francisco is fortunate in that her people are a long way yet from being overwhelmed by their architecture, no matter how powerfully the squat, massive bulk of a Federal Building may argue to the contrary. They are vocal, visible and of any and all varieties of origin, color, size and opinion; they reinforce the diversity that, if anything, has been the theme of the city's story and the framework of this appreciation. They are part of a heritage and a tradition; the San Franciscans who marched in the ranks of the Vigilance Committee in 1856, who gathered in the streets in 1910 to hear the dulcet arias of Luisa Tetrazinni, who marched with freed convict Tom Mooney down Market Street in 1939, who walked 15,000 strong down that same street in 1962 to indicate (in typically self-conscious fashion) the degree of their commitment to the principles of Human Rights Day—these San Franciscans were of separate generations and had predictably divergent concerns, but if time would allow some considerable warping, conceivably they could all stand and walk together today in one cause or another with little discernible sense of being out of time and place with each other.

The city has been the breeding ground of a strange assortment of heroes—reflections of her people. Relatively few of them, not surprisingly, have been politicians (the government belongs to the politicians, the city to the people): William C. Ralston, banker, entrepreneur, a man who overshot his mark with tremendous style; Emperor Norton, a gentle madman, "Emperor of North America and Protector of Mexico", who was supported and loved, not merely tolerated, for a quarter of a century; Dennis Kearney, sandlot orator and demagogue, one of the city's earliest labor leaders and, if a madman, not a gentle one; Adolph Sutro, who did battle with the giants of the Comstock, and won; Ambrose Bierce, a nasty-mouthed journalist and local card-carrying cynic; Mark Twain, who came and went, yet left enough of his memory that the city can still claim him as one of her own; Jack London, Tom Mooney, William Randolph Hearst, Fremont Older, Kathleen Norris, Sarah Bard Field, Abe Reuf, Paul C. Smith, Harry Bridges, Sally Stanford, "Sunny Jim" Rolph, Beniamino Bufano—novelists, poets, labor leaders, journalists, editors, a politician or two, madams, artists—a legion of the grand and the absurd. We can hope that the list will continue to grow, for the names of the city's heroes are a distillation of the uncertainties, loves, inanities, goals and integrities of the people. And the people are the city.

First, the children. A man somehow never thinks of a metropolis in terms of its children. Children belong in some other framework, in a sandlot playing baseball, climbing trees, walking along tree-shaded suburban avenues on their way to school, exploring open fields or fishing—and for all its abundance of parks, there is no mistaking the fact that San Francisco, like any other city, is mainly a matter of concrete and blacktop, a difficult and knee-scraping place in which to play. You never think of the children but you see them everywhere, and they lend their own touch of diversity and color to the city. You see them in the murky little alley-streets south of Market, gangs of them clattering down the dim streets, running you never know where. You see them on the tenement stoops of McCallister Street, small clusters of black faces, their eyes wide and not yet cynical and embittered. They will learn. You see them selling newspapers on Howard Street, and you see them on the downtown streets, whipping their bicycles in and around the hulking buses and heedless cabs; and you wonder what set of statistics is available to tell you how many are maimed in a year. You see them playing in the Civic Center, in Lafayette Park, Buena Vista Park, the Park Panhandle, totally engrossed in games whose rules you once memorized right down to your heels and forgot forever at about the age of thirteen. You see them walking to and from school past the wicked posters and beneath the bright, specific signs of Broadway's two-block miracle mile of tawdry sin, and you wonder what they think of it all, if they think of it at all. You see Mexican kids playing baseball in a rare vacant lot on Potrero Hill, Negro kids playing stickball in a side street of the Fillmore District, Chinese kids throwing a football around on a tiny school playground somewhere near Pacific Street, Italian kids in North Beach, Japanese kids on Pine Street, unclassifiable kids everywhere—and you realize that the sound of a kid hollering to have the ball thrown to him is no respecter of race, religion or present condition of servitude.

Like the children, the old men of San Francisco are seen everywhere, but you rarely think of them or of how much a part of the city scene they are. Unlike children, old men are quiet, given to sitting on benches in Union and Portsmouth Squares, faces toward the sun, hands out to the pigeons. They walk the streets and alleys south of Market, panhandling with empty eyes, gathering in little groups around the entrance to bars at six o'clock in the morning, waiting for the trip to forgetfulness to begin. They sit in the furniture of gray hotel lobbies, watching television, or just watching. They lean on the dock railings at Fisherman's Wharf, watching the boats come in; gather in North Beach for bocce-ball and arm-waving debates over the relative merits of Joe DiMaggio and Willie Mays; they sit on vegetable crates on Grant Street, reading the Chinese newspapers, making rapid Cantonese comments probably no more (or less) profound than the comments of old men anywhere; they congregate at Market and Powell, leaning against the Bank of America and criticizing the cable-car-boarding techniques of the tourists. Everywhere, the old men seek out the sun, following it around the walls of the Public Library, finding it on park benches, on the docks of the waterfront, in the streets and alleys of skid row. The old men are anywhere and everywhere. They are part of the city.

The young, the old, and the great mass of the middle—the cable-car conductors, cops and commoners, lawyers and artists, plumbers, postmen, writers, hippies, housewives and harlots, the fat, middle-aged men contemplating the marquee of a Market Street nudie movie house, the narrow young men of Montgomery Street, with their narrow young ties and tight pants, their briefcases and stockmarket minds—individually, they are no smarter, no more compassionate, possess no greater wisdom than people anywhere; they drink too much, care too little and learn not enough; but they are the people, and together they carry on the life of a city that is more than all of them.

V

"WE HAVE THUS traced the growth of San Francisco, this metropolitan prodigy, this young municipal giant, from its small and rude beginnings, through a brief career, to its present condition of magnitude and magnificence, through a record without its like elsewhere in the variety, multitude, and startling character of its impressive incidents. The city, as it now stands, is an embodiment of the highest enlightenment of our time. . . ."

This orotund assessment was rendered by historian John S. Hittell in 1878 as the conclusion to his *History of San Francisco*. That a formal history of San Francisco should have appeared less than thirty years after her emergence as a bona-fide city is not particularly surprising. Americans always have had a monumental concern for history, particularly when they felt they were making it. What is compelling about Hittell's statement, of course, is the fact that it can be used nearly a century after its writing with considerable relevance.

Even by American standards, San Francisco is still a young city; and—in spite of comparison to the sprawling behemoth of Los Angeles 400 miles to the south—who could deny that the city is still a giant? Moreover, the "variety, multitude, and startling character of its impressive incidents" continue unabated, as illustrated by the City Hall Riots of 1960, the topless revolution, the hippie invasion and a score of similarly disconcerting episodes—although, knock on wood, not yet another disaster to match that of 1906—that still compel the attention of the world. And breathes there a man with soul so dead that he will not admit that San Francisco still possesses magnitude and magnificence? If San Francisco is—and was—not quite Hittell's "embodiment of the highest enlightenment of our time", her virtues, and her faults, are still largely the result of a vigorous optimism that never quite admits of the impossible. She is a money town with the heart of a gambler; she loses quite often, but sometimes she wins, and the fact that she has never thrown in the cards and left the game may be enlightenment, of a kind.

That spirit has enabled much of the physical past to survive the pressures of the twentieth century. San Francisco has not rejected progress, but marriage between the two has not always been an untroubled cohabitation. Grand old buildings do get torn down for parking lots, and freeways continue to be built, but not without loud protest from various quarters of the city—and there is a large body of citizenry whose frequently announced goal in life is to see to it that the Embarcadero Freeway, somehow, sometime, gets dismantled, so that once again the Ferry Building will punctuate the end of Market Street like an exclamation point out of the past. A betting man would be foolish to put his money down on them—but he might be more foolish to bet against them.

That the past has not otherwise been swept completely under a twentieth-century rug is revealed in many other ways. The free-wheeling tolerance for vice and hijinks that made the Barbary Coast possible and municipal corruption grist for the journalistic mill for half a century can still be seen in the city's perennial, half-hearted attempts to clean up prostitution in the Tenderloin District and in a local political structure whose antics may or may not be entirely respectable, but are rarely dull. And if the silicone delights provided by the topless nightclubs of North Beach are pale and tinseled replicas of the city's genuinely Rabelaisan past, her gargantuan annual consumption of alcohol is in a long and venerated tradition.

There are more refined examples of the city's link to a vigorous past. Among these is her remarkably diverse population, a legacy from the gold rush-years. As of the census of 1960, the city was home to more than ten per cent of California's foreign-born population, a cosmopolitanism reflected in restaurants, newspapers and sharply defined quarters of the city where various first-, second- and third-generation nationalities tend to congregate. The most open and obvious of these is still Chinatown, a little more garish and a little less squalid than the original, but still Chinatown. And if the city will never again enjoy the visibly unchecked opulence of the Bonanza Kings, their twentieth-century corporate equivalents have erected one concrete-and-glass monument after another, testifying to their own brand of superb self-satisfaction and creating a skyline of respectable impact. The cable cars of the nineteenth century, against all logic, continue to climb hills still topped by the residences and hotels of the wealthy; ships from all the ports of the world continue to steam in and out of the Golden Gate; tourists still come by land, sea and air to see the city; and San Franciscans have persisted in the belief that while this may not be the best of all possible worlds there is no better place on earth to endure it than in the city by the western gate.

She is still a city of beauty, a city of hills and wind and water; she is still a city of style, grace, wit and that splendid provincialism that provides a man with identity of place; she is still a city of people capable of viewing themselves as somehow different, perhaps a little ridiculous occasionally, but not always afraid to admit it; a city in which time is sometimes forced to stand still—and time has always been the final enemy, as poet Gelett Burgess remarked long ago: "Time alone can tame the town, rob it of its nameless charm, subdue it to the Commonplace. May time be merciful—may it delay its fatal duty till we have learned that to love, to forgive, to enjoy, is but to understand!"

Time has not yet done its work; perhaps it never will.

THE PLATES

GHIRARDELLI SQUARE, LARKIN AND BEACH STREETS

The "city that knows how" hasn't *always* known how, and sometimes it hasn't known how in spectacular fashion—while creating an Embarcadero Freeway, for example. Fortunately for the city's reputation, however, free enterprise has occasionally managed to offset the city's frequent lapses. Such is the case with Ghirardelli Square, which demonstrates that unique sense of style that has enabled the city to survive the sometimes repellent demands of progress. Designed and constructed from a core of antiquated buildings once owned by the Ghirardelli Chocolate Factory, the Square is a rubbernecker's delight of curio emporiums, dress shops, restaurants and taverns, complete with balcony dining areas, tinkling fountains and an admirable view of the Municipal Pier, its lagoon, the Bay and Alcatraz Island, whose snout is poking into the upper right-hand corner of the picture.

STAIRSTEP ARCHITECTURE, TELEGRAPH HILL

The houses and apartments of Telegraph Hill are terraced like boxes stacked in a supermarket, rambling over the hill's roller-coaster topography in violation of basic physical laws. Seen here, past and present mingle in uneasy co-existence, the clapboard-and-shingle oldtimers snuggling shoulder-to-shoulder in defense against the raucous newcomer above them. The scene is symptomatic of San Francisco, for Telegraph Hill is awash with memories—memories of the days when a massive signal tower stood here to mark the entrance of mail ships for the anxious eyes of home-hungry goldseekers; of the days when Italian immigrants clustered the hill in Mediterranean exuberance; of the days not long past when the hill was a refuge for sundry painters and ravenous *literati* who provided perhaps the last link to an age in which Bohemianism was a state of grace. Today, along with the flat-topped apartments, has come a new generation of beautiful young people, secretaries, lawyers, executives and swingers who perhaps have forgotten the style of the past but may be creating a style of their own—who knows? Above it all, the snub-nosed tip of Coit Tower (see page 92) rises 210 feet above contrast and contention.

34

CITY, SEA AND SKY: A VIEW FROM TIBURON

Poet George Sterling's "cool, gray city of love" dominates the horizon from whatever vantage-point she is seen; it is the secret of her drama and her appeal. Whether dimmed in summer haze or—as seen here—washed white by the sun and wind-whipped into stunning clarity, the city's beauty is imperishable. She mantles herself in light and air like a woman trying on opera gowns in a Union Square shop, and if it sometimes seems as though she cannot make up her mind, like any other woman, it doesn't really matter; her taste is impeccable.

THE LAST OF THE CAPE HORNERS, PIER 43

The working history of the square-rigged *Balclutha* is a narrative in miniature of much of the great days of maritime trade on the Pacific Coast. Clyde-built and launched in Glasgow, Scotland, in 1886, she was a "deepwaterman" typical of the period: steel-hulled, she was 256.5 feet long, with a beam of 38.6 feet and a depth of 22.7 feet; her mainmast rose 145 feet from the deck and her measure was 1689 gross tons. Her maiden voyage was around the Horn to San Francisco, where she joined the mighty fleet of grain traders of the 1880s. From then until her purchase by the San Francisco Maritime Museum Association in 1954, she served a varied career as Australia lumberman, Calcutta jute-carrier, Alaska Packers Fleet member under the pseudonym *Star of Alaska*, movie prop and roving sea museum known as the *Pacific Queen*. In 1955, the San Francisco Maritime Museum completed an immense job of restoration and re-christened her *Balclutha*. On display at Pier 43, Fisherman's Wharf, the last of the Cape Horn traders is open to the public, a living reminder of the city's vigorous maritime past.

THE CRAB SELECTION, FISHERMAN'S WHARF

Fisherman's Wharf, lying two blocks north of the terminus of the Powell Street cable-car line, is a clamorous mixture of that peculiarly twentieth-century commercialism known as the tourist trade and an honorable profession whose origins are lost in prehistory. For more than a century the center of the commercial fishing industry in the Bay Area, the Wharf has accumulated through the years such curious appendages as knick-knack shops offering ash trays made of genuine redwood, ash trays made of genuine abalone shells and genuine plastic wall mottoes; restaurants whose ethnic themes range from German schmaltz to Italian provincial; a wax museum, hot-dog stands, open-air fish cafeterias, chandleries, balloon stands and—nearby—an enormous import store where a man can purchase an authentic Watutsi lion-spear, if he cares to do such a thing. But above all, the Wharf is a fish-lover's paradise providing a wide selection of briny delights—including still-squirming crabs plucked from the deep during the harvesting season between mid-November and the end of May. They also can be bought dead, if preferred.

40

BONGOES AT THE BEACH, AQUATIC PARK

A crowd out for a Sunday frolic is entertained by an impromptu bongo concert. Although the topless young man in the center seems to be doing all right, the vagaries of San Francisco's climate do not often allow for the kind of sun-worshiping that can be seen in, say, Pismo Beach. There is not a bikini in sight here, but not very many years ago, when San Francisco pioneered the use of the topless bathing suit, it would not have been surprising to see one or more goose-pimpled young ladies braving pneumonia for the sake of social revolution. The crowds were significantly larger, then. Nestled against the Hyde Street Pier across the lagoon are three floating museums. The ship at the left is the steam schooner *Wapama*, which once navigated the dogholes of the Pacific Coast from San Francisco to Puget Sound. In the center is the ferryboat *Eureka*, a massive relic of the Sausalito run. The three-masted schooner at the right is the *C. A. Thayer*, the last of a grand breed of ships that once plied the bleak waters off Alaska as part of the codfishing fleet. All three ships have been superbly restored and are open to the public under the auspices of the State Park system. They are pungent artifacts of an age that knew neither bongo concerts nor—most assuredly—topless bathing suits.

FORT WINFIELD SCOTT, PRESIDIO

With a wide view of the Golden Gate and the Marin headlands, Fort Winfield Scott occupies the cliffs at the northwest corner of the San Francisco Presidio. Work on the fort was begun in 1905 and for several years her batteries provided the mainstay of San Francisco's Harbor defense in an era in which all you needed for protection against an enemy were some big guns. The opportunity for using the guns in anger never presented itself, however, and the fort is today abandoned, her impressive battlements rendered obsolete by the age of ICBMs and pushbutton annihilation.

THE BRIDGE ACROSS CHRYSOPYLAE

In 1846, John Charles Frémont paused in his "conquest" of California long enough to dub the entrance to the Bay of San Francisco "Chrysopylae"— Gate of Gold. The name stuck, and was given to the bridge that spanned it ninety years later. Begun in 1931, the Golden Gate Bridge was opened to traffic on May 25, 1937. Its construction was a stupendous engineering feat, as a few statistics will illustrate: each of the two towers rises 746 feet above the water; its full length is 8940 feet and the distance between the towers is 4200 feet—a record until the construction of New York's Verrazano Narrows Bridge; the six lanes of the bridge's roadbed are 220 feet above the water, and the cables that support it are more than three feet in diameter and comprised of 27,572 individual strands of steel cable. Another interesting statistic is the fact that more than 300 people have jumped to their deaths from the bridge since its construction, most of them from the Bay, or San Francisco, side. Sentimentalists claim they do this so that their last sight is of San Francisco; cynics maintain that the jumpers are afraid to cross over to the ocean side—a man could get killed in the traffic.

UNIVERSITY OF SAN FRANCISCO

Framed by the pines of San Francisco Overlook, the twin spires of the University of San Francisco dominate the cityscape of Lone Mountain. The elegant air of Spanish Revival sported by this Catholic institution has an air of architectural flamboyance that has added much to the flavor of the city's skyline. Together with the nearby San Francisco College for Women, San Francisco State College, San Francisco City College, and sundry extensions of the University of California, the University of San Francisco carries on the educational heritage of a city whose first attempt at a formal school was a crude shanty on Portsmouth Plaza—the Public Institute School, founded in 1848 and attended by some thirty or forty children.

JAPANESE TEA GARDEN, GOLDEN GATE PARK

In 1871, William Hammond Hall began a project designed to transform a 1017-acre rectangle of wind-ridden sand dunes into San Francisco's largest city park. Its name was Golden Gate Park, and after John McLaren took over its maintenance in 1890, it soon gained a well-deserved reputation as one of the most beautiful city parks in the country. McLaren, a transplanted Scotsman with a messianic zeal for the qualities of nature, remained park superintendent until his death in 1943, and during his lifetime managed to integrate into his park no less than 300 varieties of rhododendron and 100 varieties of eucalyptus; it is said that he planted more than a million trees. The Japanese Tea Garden, located at the eastern end of the park, was first built as a part of the city's Mid-Winter Fair of 1894, and has since been expanded; it is comprised of a tea house, a gift shop, a small five-roofed pagoda, nearly three acres of magnificent gardens with pools, streams, paths and miniature bridges, and "the Buddha that sits through sunny and rainy weather without shade"—an eleven-foot statue cast in Tajima Province, Japan, in 1790. Golden Gate Park's other features include an aquarium, a planetarium, an art museum, a polo field, riding trails, bicycle paths, lakes, tiny herds of buffalo and Kezar Stadium, where the San Francisco 49ers lose to the Los Angeles Rams with masochistic regularity.

THE EMPEROR'S BRIDGE

With solemn decree, Emperor Norton conceived and ordained the San Francisco–Oakland Bay Bridge nearly one hundred years ago: "*Now, therefore*, we, Norton I, Emperor of the United States and protector of Mexico, do order and direct . . . that a suspension bridge be constructed from . . . Oakland Point to Yerba Buena [San Francisco], from thence to the mountain range of Sausalito, and from thence to the Farallones. . . ." The Emperor's orders were finally carried out in 1936, but there was obvious malfeasance on someone's part. The 8½-mile bridge between Oakland and San Francisco certainly adhered to the Emperor's brilliant plan—although it departed somewhat by using Yerba Buena Island as a link between the two cities—and it might be said that the Golden Gate Bridge comprised an extension "to the mountain range of Sausalito", but the Emperor's bridge has not been completed from Sausalito to the Farallones, a tiny island group lying more than twenty miles at sea. Perhaps the engineers ran out of money; perhaps someone lost the blueprints; perhaps no one *wanted* to drive to the Farallones—at any rate, the potentate's grand design has not been finished. The Emperor would not be amused.

THE NORTH BAY FROM TAMALPAIS

Mount Tamalpais stands in triangulated splendor north of San Francisco, a green, wooded wonderland that is a view in itself and whose flanks provide such spectacular vistas of the Bay as that shown. In the center of the picture is Richardson Bay, an appendage separated from the rest of the Bay by the Tiburon Peninsula, and beyond that is Angel Island, to the north of which thin tendrils of fog slither over the hills. In the immediate foreground of the picture are the greensward and "bleachers" of the Cushing Outdoor Theater.

RHODODENDRON SKYLINE, FROM TWIN PEAKS

Looking north and east from a rhododendron patch on Twin Peaks, the roller-coaster inclinations of the city are superbly illustrated. The precise number of hills in San Francisco has never been ascertained with unchallenged finality. One of the latest counts has it that there are forty-two. Tourists from the flatland prairies have been known to maintain, after a day of walking, that there could not be less than 138. Classicists hold that there are only seven legitimate hills, thereby lending authority to the idea that San Francisco enjoys an emotional kinship with Rome. In the center of the picture is a lump over which no one cares to argue: Buena Vista Hill, topped by a thirty-seven-acre park established in 1894. Just beyond the hill can be seen the squarish hulk of the Federal Office Building looming (symbolically?) over the dome of City Hall.

MISSION DOLORES, 16TH AND DOLORES STREETS

One of the two surviving relics of San Francisco's short-lived Spanish period, Mission Dolores is overshadowed today by the parish church built next to it in 1916, yet holds its own as one of the more individualistic structures in the city. It was begun in 1782 and completed in 1791, fifteen years after Juan Bautista de Anza led the first Spanish settlers north from Sonora, Mexico, to the Bay of San Francisco. To the left of the Mission building (and out of sight) is a tiny cemetery that houses the earthly remains of such disparate luminaries of the city's past as Don Francisco de Haro, first alcalde of San Francisco, William Leidesdorff, Negro merchant and pioneer, and James P. Casey and Charles Cora, whose necks were stretched by the Committee of Vigilance in 1856.

END OF THE HYDE STREET LINE, AQUATIC PARK

To half the world and his wife, San Francisco means cable car, and cable car means San Francisco. The persistence with which this outlandish little vehicle has managed to survive the vicissitudes of time would doubtless warm the cockles of its inventor, Andrew S. Hallidie, who first put it through its paces in 1873. Slow, impractical, unutterably charming, the cable car continues to flout gravity with a style more or less immortalized by poet Gelett Burgess at the turn of the century:

North Beach to Tenderloin, over Russian Hill,
The grades are something giddy and the curves are fit to kill!
All the way to Market Street, climbing up the slope,
Down upon the other side, hanging to the rope;
But the sight of San Francisco as you take the lurching dip!
There is plenty of excitement, on the Hyde Street Grip!

Oh, the lights are in the Mission and the ships are in the Bay;
And Tamalpais is looming from the Gate across the way;
The Presidio trees are waving and the hills are growing brown!
And the driving fog is harried from the Ocean to the town!
How the pulleys slap and rattle! How the cables hum and whip!
Oh, they sing a gallant chorus on the Hyde Street Grip!

THE WORKINGMAN'S WHARF

Behind all the garish neon clutter of restaurants and gew-gaw emporiums, Fisherman's Wharf remains a working community whose trade is fishing, whose ties to the Bay and the sea beyond have remained unbroken for more than a century. The technology of fishing has become sophisticated but these craft, and the men who own and operate them, can trace their lineage in fact and spirit to the days of lateen-rigged sail, when one of the most compelling sights in the city's daily life was the pre-dawn exodus of its Italian fishing fleet as it slipped out of the Golden Gate, bound for crops off the north and west coast.

EMPIRE WEST: KAISER CENTER, OAKLAND

For years, the Eastbay skyline was dominated by the two buildings that some would have said effectively bracketed the power structure of Oakland: the towering baroque edifice housing the *Oakland Tribune*, and the more restrained architecture of City Hall. That balance was disrupted in 1960, when the twenty-eight-story Kaiser Center rose from the shores of Lake Merritt. The building is the headquarters of Kaiser Industries and its multitudinous subsidiaries around the world, the core of an empire begun by Henry J. Kaiser in the early 1920s. The building symbolizes Oakland's emergence as a leading financial and industrial complex on the Pacific Coast. Lake Merritt itself provides an effective antidote to all this frenetic commercialism, offering sailboating privileges, an impressive city park, a wildfowl refuge, a small zoo and Fairyland, a delightful fantasy for children.

CASTAWAY, SAN FRANCISCO BEACH

One of the most ubiquitous sights on the California coast from San Diego to Cape Mendocino is the isolated surf fisherman pitting skill and persistence against the breaking sea. The surf fisherman is one of a hard and lonely breed whose dedication to the requirements of his part-time trade is matched only by the devout dry-fly fisherman. This individual is trying the surf of San Francisco Beach. He may spend the entire day hauling in 200-pound clumps of kelp; he may lose his tackle four or five times; he probably will get sun- and wind-burned and arm-weary from repeated casting; he may not catch a thing—none of it really matters. He is alone and unhampered by the demands and worries of his workday week. Here, there is nothing but the sound of the sea, the wind and the peevish squawk of the gull as it tries to steal his bait.

INSCRUTABLE CONFECTION: CHINATOWN

If the colorful façade of Grant Street, seen here, bears a remarkable family resemblance to something the prop men of MGM might have whipped up, the similarity is not entirely coincidental. Grant Street, the commercial heart of Chinatown, is an eight-block confection of Oriental shops, restaurants and bars whose entire *raison d'être* is to titillate tourists and provide the Caucasian San Franciscan with that smug sense of cosmopolitanism his soul craves. The census of 1960 reported that there were 36,445 Chinese and Chinese-Americans in San Francisco, most of them clustered in and about the confines of Chinatown. As in most of the rest of American society, the indisputable wealth of the Chinatown business community has not exactly filtered down in equal proportion to the bulk of the district's population, which lives in often overcrowded, substandard housing and makes a living sometimes at wages beyond belief. But Chinatown goes on, one of the oldest and most magnetic of the city's attractions, offering unarguably good food, incomparable smells, delicate importations of jewelry, lacquered furniture, ivory carvings and sundry other Oriental delights manufactured in Hong Kong, Japan, Taiwan, India and East Orange, New Jersey. It is not called a ghetto; it is not called a slum; it is called Chinatown.

DEFINITIVE SAN FRANCISCO: GRANT AVENUE AND CALIFORNIA STREET

In many ways, the intersection of Grant Avenue and California Street makes eminently visible the structural vicissitudes of a town capable of promoting and resisting change simultaneously. California Street, here seen sporting a cable car, intersects the glittering heart of Chinatown, but carries on very little of the district's peculiar flavor—a flavor marked especially by what some of its more skeptical Chinese residents call "pigtail architecture". On the northeast corner of the intersection (not visible here) is Old St. Mary's Church, a distinctly occidental Catholic Church whose red brick and granite lines are almost overpowered by the convoluted neon pagodas all around it. The pagodas, in turn, are put in the shade of the immense International Building, a structure that positively shouts modernity and progress and the "go-ahead" confidence of occidental enterprise. The heavy-handed symbolism of the whole scene is capped by the sight of a nineteenth-century cable car crossing Grant Street—a thoroughfare never meant for twentieth-century traffic and therefore irresistible to knuckleheaded drivers.

ENCHANTED RELIC: THE PALACE OF FINE ARTS

It was generally maintained that Bernard Maybeck, an architect who designed scores upon scores of Bay Area structures, surpassed his own genius when he came up with the Palace of Fine Arts for the Panama-Pacific International Exposition of 1915. A magnificent blend of the neo-Classicism of the time and a baroque melancholy provided by its lagoon setting, the Palace inspired such unrestrained admiration as that uttered by poet Edwin Markham, who bluntly proclaimed that it was the most beautiful structure in the history of mankind. Few cared to argue, and when all the other buildings were torn down after the Exposition, the Palace remained, an enchanted relic of the age of innocence. Unhappily, the Palace—never designed to last forever—was badly used by time and weather; its imitation-travertine marble steadily deteriorated through the years, until by the mid-1950s it was in real danger of total disintegration, great chunks falling from its pediments, and heads, arms and legs separating themselves from the grand female torsos of Ulrich Ellerhusen. So San Francisco—being San Francisco—the state of California, and local philanthropist Walter Johnson came up with 7.4 million dollars to restore the buildings of the Palace (now complete). The whole business of restoration was a magnificent display of stubborn impracticality; after all, 7.4 million dollars *might* have built as much as fifty feet of double-decked freeway.

72

SPORTING TYPES, SAN FRANCISCO BAY

Trifling with the sea, in one form or another, has been a favorite San Francisco pastime for more than a century, and yachting an organized sport since the formation of the San Francisco Yacht Club in 1869, one of the earliest such organizations in the United States. Once the exclusive province of those who could afford the time and money involved, organized and unorganized sailing for pleasure by now has become thoroughly democratized, and a brisk summer's Sunday will find the Bay an absolute welter of sloops and yawls, ketches and schooners—and an occasional catboat or El Toro poking its tiny bow out of the relative safety of one Bay harbor or another, its master intent on conquering mother sea. Remarkably few of them drown.

74

MUNICIPAL YACHT HARBOR

San Francisco's Municipal Yacht Harbor, one of more than twenty-five such in the Bay Area, offers several hundred berths for the weekend sailor. The Harbor also possesses the city's two major yacht clubs, the St. Francis and the Golden Gate—although there are many other clubs scattered around the Bay, including the San Francisco Yacht Club at Belvedere and the Corinthian Yacht Club at Corinthian Island, Tiburon. While sailing goes on most of the year, the "official" season begins on the first Sunday in May and continues through the next five months, with many splendid competitions featuring boats ranging in size and style from the thirty-eight-foot Farallone Clippers to the eight-foot El Toros, a design originated in the Bay Area. Inboard and outboard power craft also are popular, and in a fashion not unique to the Bay Area sailors and power-boat skippers tend to look upon one another with good-natured disdain.

SAN FRANCISCO CITY HALL, CIVIC CENTER

The crowning glory of San Francisco's Civic Center complex (which includes such other massive structures as Exposition Auditorium, the Public Library, the War Memorial Opera House and the Veterans Memorial Building) is the City Hall, an immense building that occupies an area covering two city blocks. Designed by John Bakewell, Jr., and Arthur Brown, Jr., the City Hall was constructed of native granite in 1915 as the largest and last of several city halls in San Francisco's history. The building that preceded it was fairly impressive itself; unfortunately (after taking twenty-five curious years to build), it was also the only major building in the city to be demolished by the earthquake alone in 1906— a fact that gave rise to some speculation as to the competence of its builders and the honesty of the politicians who had hired them. At any rate, the present City Hall was a complete Renaissance success, and a particular point of local pride is the fact that the 308-foot dome is sixteen feet, three inches higher than that of the national capitol in Washington. It has not been noted whether Washington has given the matter much thought.

PLEASE KEEP
ON THE WALKS

SUMMER SKYLINE: A VIEW FROM THE GOLDEN GATE BRIDGE

A striking peculiarity of San Francisco's summers is the soft, billowing river of fog that ebbs and flows through the Golden Gate with almost tidal regularity. It is the natural air conditioning that makes San Francisco one of the few American cities endurable in the summer months. Moreover, it contributes mightily to the city's fickle, shifting personality. The still-bright skyline, seen here from the north end of the Golden Gate Bridge, soon will be dimmed and muffled, and the city will become a vague, mist-ridden Atlantis where sounds have the disconnectedness of dreams and the hollow growling of the foghorns gives it all the melancholy and faintly menacing air of an old Humphrey Bogart movie.

THE SPIRAL GARDENS OF LOMBARD STREET

San Francisco is a city filled with sudden curiosities, but few are more startling than the first sight and negotiation of this one-block section of Lombard Street on Russian Hill—a brick-paved corkscrew whose sumptuous hydrangea landscaping might be reminiscent of the hanging gardens of Babylon, were there anyone around to remember the hanging gardens of Babylon. The gardens of Lombard Street definitely will be remembered, particularly by adventurous tourists who have already been unnerved by driving up and down the city's forty-two hills. Some of these stricken types have been known to crawl down Lombard Street with eyes completely shut—and never hit a parked car or a flower. God watches over them.

THE GENTEEL BATTLEGROUND OF RUSSIAN HILL

Thrusting impertinently from a sea of Victorian Italianate, the modern high-rise condominiums of Russian Hill have permanently altered a hilltop skyline formerly reminiscent of a genteel Bohemian tradition. Once the habitat of such turn-of-the-century literary and artistic lights as Ina Coolbrith, Frank and Kathleen Norris, Gelett Burgess, George Sterling, Peter B. Kyne, Willis Polk and Douglas Tilden, Russian Hill has slowly evolved from artistic colony to fashionable residential district and now to condominium complex. The process has not taken place free of bitterness, however; residents not fortunate enough to live in the mighty apartment buildings have been heard to complain that they constitute a kind of Chinese Wall against the view, and a vigorous and eminently vocal opposition continues to greet further development along these lines.

BRAVING THE GALES OF LAKE MERRITT, OAKLAND

San Francisco tends to look upon her sister city of Oakland with the disdain a seventh-generation dowager might convey upon a *nouveau-riche* family. The inferiority implied in such an attitude, however, has not kept Oakland from developing one of the best city park systems in the country; it has not kept her from funding and constructing a magnificent museum complex; nor has it prevented her from controlling hot-eyed developers who would dearly love to mutilate the attractive landscape in and about Lake Merritt, a downtown recreational center that provides a swatch of open space, water and greenery in the midst of urban clutter. Sailing is prominent on the lake, and such miniature regattas as this one match the enthusiasm—if not the size and quantity—of the fleets of the Bay itself.

86

THE RAREFIED DELIGHTS OF NOB HILL

Nob Hill, the geographic and psychological pinnacle of San Francisco's Establishment, is so unabashedly affluent that its very arrogance lends the entire city much of its style—and if there is something besides the cable car that is immediately identifiable the world over as a representation of San Francisco, it is this cool and windswept enclave of the superbly well-to-do. Shown here is the Mark Hopkins Hotel ("The Mark" to natives) at the right, constructed in 1926 on the site of the mansion of Mark Hopkins, one of the "Big Four" memorialized in song, story and critical history textbook. At a diagonal across California Street from the Mark is the James Flood mansion, the only one of the old Nob Hill mansions to survive the fire of 1906. It was constructed of Eastern brownstone and today houses the Pacific Union Club, a men's organization so exclusive that it is limited to 100 members. Behind the Flood mansion is the Fairmont Hotel, built in 1907 and featuring today a garish twenty-nine-story tower with an outside elevator some call the "thermometer". Huntington Park, one of the smallest and most delightful in the city, is in the center foreground.

UNIVERSITY OF CALIFORNIA, BERKELEY

Founded in 1868, the University of California has grown from two buildings and an enrollment of less than fifty students to an immense, statewide
multiversity whose Berkeley campus alone had a fall 1967 enrollment of
more than 27,000 and an operating budget that topped forty-five million
dollars. The outstanding landmark on the Berkeley campus is the towering
Camponile, a bell tower erected in 1914 by Jane K. Sather in memory of
her husband. The tower has a carillon of twelve bells that rings out the
hours and occasional incidental music during the day. An elevator to the
top of the Camponile provides access to a stupendous view of the East Bay.
The formerly open observation windows were enclosed in thick slabs of
glass some time ago, since despairing students were beginning to look
upon the tower as a convenient substitute for the Golden Gate Bridge. One
of the most impressive experiences available in the East Bay is to stand in
the observation room when the great bells sound the hours.

A LEGACY FROM FIREBELL LILLIE,
WASHINGTON SQUARE

This subdued monument to San Francisco's volunteer firemen in no way hints at the untrammeled exuberance of the woman who caused its construction. Lillie Hitchcock Coit came to San Francisco in 1851 as a child of eight and remained to become one of the town's most beautiful socialites, "a phantom of delight", as one of the papers put it, given to such unrefined antics as chasing after fires, smoking cigarettes in and out of public, drinking hand-to-fist with the best of men, playing poker—and winning, attending cock fights and using language of a variety and muscularity that would strike envy into the black heart of a jerk-line teamster. Of all her pursuits, however, nothing was dearer to her wild heart than attending a fire. Volunteer Engine Company Knickerbocker No. 5 was her favorite from childhood, and in 1863 the Company made her an Honorary Member, a testimonial she cherished possibly as much as she did her long marriage to Benjamin Howard Coit, chairman of the San Francisco Stock Board. Lillie lived on in her extraordinary fashion until 1928; upon her death, a sum of $118,000 was bequeathed for the beautification of the city, resulting in Coit Tower (see page 34), and a smaller sum was allocated for the erection of this modest tribute to the fire department she loved.

URBAN OASIS: UNION SQUARE

Union Square, a wide space of greenery set down in the center of the city's clattering commercial heart, has been an unofficial civic center for more than a century. Taking its name from the pro-Union gatherings held here immediately preceding the Civil War, the square has remained a staging area for meetings whose purposes have varied from bitter protest to official celebrations of one kind or another, including "Rhododendron Week". The bronze figure of Victory poised ethereally atop the granite shaft at left was erected in commemoration of Admiral Dewey's destruction of the Spanish fleet at Manila in 1898; the square's population of profligate pigeons also finds it attractive. Surrounded on four sides by massive, neo-Renaissance buildings and grand street-level shops selling everything from airline tickets to Oleg Cassini originals, Union Square is a particularly effective representation of the serene elegance that still personifies the cool, gray city by the western gate.